Monitoring Terrestrial Reptiles and Amphibians in the Mediterranean Coast Network, 2009 Project Report

Santa Monica Mountains National Recreation Area, Cabrillo National Monument, and Channel Islands National Park

Natural Resource Data Series NPS/MEDN/NRDS—2011/135

Kathleen Semple Delaney and Seth P. D. Riley

National Park Service
Santa Monica Mountains National Recreation Area
401 W. Hillcrest Dr.
Thousand Oaks, CA 91360

Lena Lee and Stacey Ostermann-Kelm

Mediterranean Coast Network
National Park Service Inventory and Monitoring Program
401 W. Hillcrest Dr.
Thousand Oaks, CA 91360

Benjamin Pister

National Park Service
Cabrillo National Monument
1800 Cabrillo Memorial Dr.
San Diego, CA 92106

Helen Fitting

National Park Service
Channel Islands National Park
1901 Spinnaker Dr.
Ventura, CA 93001

February 2011

U.S. Department of the Interior
National Park Service
Natural Resource Program Center
Fort Collins, Colorado

The National Park Service, Natural Resource Program Center publishes a range of reports that address natural resource topics of interest and applicability to a broad audience in the National Park Service and others in natural resource management, including scientists, conservation and environmental constituencies, and the public.

The Natural Resource Data Series is intended for the timely release of basic data sets and data summaries. Care has been taken to assure accuracy of raw data values, but a thorough analysis and interpretation of the data has not been completed. Consequently, the initial analyses of data in this report are provisional and subject to change.

All manuscripts in the series receive the appropriate level of peer review to ensure that the information is scientifically credible, technically accurate, appropriately written for the intended audience, and designed and published in a professional manner.

This report received informal peer review by subject-matter experts who were not directly involved in the collection, analysis, or reporting of the data.

Views, statements, findings, conclusions, recommendations, and data in this report do not necessarily reflect views and policies of the National Park Service, U.S. Department of the Interior. Mention of trade names or commercial products does not constitute endorsement or recommendation for use by the U.S. Government.

This report is available from the Natural Resource Publications Management website (http://www.nature.nps.gov/publications/nrpm/).

Please cite this publication as:

NPS 638/106545, 342/106545, 159/106545, February 2011

Contents

Contents (continued)

Figures

Figures (continued)

Tables

Acknowledgments

We thank the following interns and staff for providing field assistance at Santa Monica Mountains National Recreation Area (SAMO): Seth Riley, Joanne Moriarty, Cathy Schoonmaker, Jenna Dodge, Andrew Valand, Rachel Lopez, Julie Golla, David Percival, Mike Robinson, Leah Card, and Keely Craig.

At Cabrillo National Monument (CABR), the following Volunteers-in-Parks provided assistance in the field: Nancy Arthur-McGahee, Ryan Baker-Branstetter, Mary Ryan Barthel, Talesa Bleything, Ian Cain, Nick Cates, Amye Sue Cherundolo, Emily Clayton, Shannon Coates, Andrea Cook, sarah Cox, Dan Della-Rocco, Jim Diermeier, Jenna Dodge, Mike Hamilton, Leslie Handa, Daniel Hartsook, Darcy Hayes, Julia Kuhns, Kelly Lion, Tristan Loper, Ben Lucas, Joe McKenna, Lisa Miller, Brian Palo, Kathleen Pangan, Heather Rothbard, John Skoglund, Julia Smith, Bill Taylor, and Jim Thornley. We also thank the following CABR staff who provided assistance or leadership in the field: Andrea Compton, Amanda Gossard, Neil Heller, Taylor Jordan, Krystal Tronboll, and Tracey Mueller-Gibbs. Special thanks to SAMO staff and interns, Jenna Dodge, Lauren Ross, Cathy Schoonmaker, and Andrew Valand for helping Cabrillo during staffing shortages.

We are grateful for field assistance at Channel Islands National Park from the following members of the island fox crew: Jen Savage, Jim Howard, Sara Hansen, and Angela Guglielmino. Shenandoah Marr also provided invaluable field assistance through the Volunteers-in-Parks program. Charles Drost (USGS) provided field assistance and generously shared his expertise on the herpetofauna of the Channel Islands. We thank Dr. Cathy Schwemm and her students at California State University Channel Islands for replacing old cover boards on East Anacapa Island. We extend special thanks to Tim Coonan (CHIS) for providing valuable help with database queries and reviewing this report.

Funding for monitoring was provided by the Mediterranean Coast Inventory and Monitoring Network, Cabrillo National Monument, Santa Monica Mountains National Recreation Area and Channel Islands National Park.

Introduction

Reptiles and amphibians in the parks of the Mediterranean Coast Network (MEDN) of the Inventory and Monitoring Program in Southern California are affected by numerous stressors and impacts to their environment and habitat. Global fluctuations in temperature, increased exposure to ultraviolet radiation, interaction with exotic species, and changes in air and water quality have all been linked to declines in lizard and amphibian populations (c.f. Blaustein & Wake 1990; Sinervo et al. 2010). In addition, urban development has significantly altered or destroyed critical habitat for many reptile and amphibian species. This is especially so at Santa Monica Mountains National Recreation Area (SAMO) and Cabrillo National Monument (CABR). Seven of the nineteen species of herpetofauna historically known to occur on the Point Loma peninsula in San Diego, California and CABR are now thought to have been extirpated (Atkinson et al. 2003). Eleven of the 34 species of herpetofauna found in the Santa Monica Mountains are listed as rare, threatened or endangered by the California Department of Fish and Game (CDFG) or the U.S. Fish and Wildlife Service (USFWS). Seven additional species are species of concern for the National Park Service. Evaluation of historic data along with some recent studies suggests that a number of reptile species in the Santa Monica Mountains are in decline (NPS unpublished data; De Lisle et al. 1986; Gamradt & Kats 1996, 1997). Much of this information, however, is insufficient to determine the actual or potential impacts of expanding urbanization in southern California.

While Channel Islands National Park (CHIS) supports nine herptile species on the five islands that comprise the park, the monitoring program focuses on three of the five species found on Anacapa Island, Santa Barbara Island, and San Miguel Island. Two of the three monitored species, the island night lizard (*Xantusia riversiana*) and Channel Islands slender salamander (*Batrachoseps pacificus*), are endemic to the Channel Islands. The island night lizard was federally listed as threatened due to predation from feral cats (*Felis catus*) and habitat modification from feral goats (*Capra hircus*) and feral pigs (*Sus scrofa*) (USFWS 1976, 41 FR 22073 22075). The Channel Islands slender salamander is a federal species of concern. The third monitored species at CHIS is the southern alligator lizard (*Elgaria multicarinata*). Island fence lizards (*Sceloporus occidentalis becki*) and side-blotched lizards (*Uta stansburiana*) are found on the 3 islands that are included in this monitoring program, but they are not readily captured by the cover board technique and so minimal data are collected for these species. Impacts to amphibians and reptiles on the Channel Islands are primarily related to the effects of introduced non-native species.

Long-term monitoring objectives for CABR and SAMO include determining the status and trend in: (1) annual occupancy, (2) community dynamics (species richness, evenness, and extinction and colonization rates), and (3) capture rates for herpetofaunal species in selected vegetation communities. Species richness has been suggested as a good indicator of ecosystem quality and integrity for reptiles because of the group's broad diversity, habitat requirements, and diet specificity. Additionally, distribution and abundance information is critical for the design of restoration strategies and land management programs to protect or recover reptile and amphibian populations from decline. This information is invaluable to NPS resource managers in evaluating the ecological health of these important indicator species and of the broader ecosystem.

Long-term objectives for herptile monitoring at CHIS include two measures of population status: 1) an uncalibrated index of population size, and 2) a weight-length regression. The population index allows the park to roughly track changes in population size and document long-term trends and sudden, short term changes. The weight-length regression provides a measure of the general health of individuals in the population.

This report summarizes the monitoring of terrestrial reptiles and amphibians conducted in 2009 within the 3 MEDN parks: CABR, SAMO, and CHIS. Here we provide only simple summary statistics, but future analyses will directly address the objectives of the protocol such as determining the status and trends of herptofaunal occupancy rates, community dynamics, and abundance indices.

Methods

The methods and procedures used in SAMO and CABR during the 2009 field season followed Busteed et al. (2006). Details of the field sampling and data analysis methods are provided below. Herpetofaunal monitoring at CHIS was performed following the general procedures described by Fellers et al. (1988). Since its inception 17 years ago, the CHIS program has been modified several times; four annual reports have been written to date and each contains descriptions of changes to the protocol (Schwemm 1995; Schwemm 1996; Austin 1996; Austin 1998).

Brief history of monitoring efforts

Monitoring of terrestrial reptile and amphibian species distribution and abundance has been ongoing in CHIS since 1993 (CHIS Tech Report 98-03) and in Point Loma Ecological Area (PLECA)which includes CABR in San Diego since 1995 (Brown & Fisher 2002). CHIS monitoring was conducted by park staff following the methods described by Fellers et al. (1988). PLECA monitoring was initiated and conducted by staff from the United States Geological Survey (USGS), Western Ecological Research Center (WERC) following a generic protocol for monitoring herpetofauna using pitfall traps (Stokes et al. 2001). The regional significance of reptiles and amphibians as indicators of ecosystem health lead to initiation of similar monitoring in the broader Santa Monica Mountains ecosystem early in the monitoring planning process in 2000. CABR staff took over monitoring of the PLECA in 2000, although USGS continues very similar monitoring throughout San Diego County.

Field sampling

Because of their small size, cryptic coloration, and nocturnal or fossorial behavior, effective sampling of reptile and amphibian populations can be difficult, and many techniques have been developed to assess the diversity and abundance of these species. Of the various methods tested, pitfall trapping with supplemental funnel snake-traps has been found to be an effective sampling methodology (Case & Fisher 2001; Fisher & Case 2000a, b).

Pitfall trapping consists of the deployment of a series of sampling arrays that are based on the premise that ambulatory reptiles and amphibians can be directed by "drift" fences into bucket traps (pits) embedded in the ground. In this design each pitfall array consists of seven 5-gallon buckets buried so that the lip of the bucket is flush with the surface of the ground to serve as a "pitfall" (Campbell & Christman 1982; Corn 1994; Fisher & Case 2000b; Fisher et al. 2002). Buried buckets are situated approximately 7.5 meters apart along a "Y" configured drift fence. There are two buckets along each arm and one at the vertex of the three arms. Snake traps are placed along each arm of the drift fence. Drift fences intercept reptiles and amphibians directing them into either pitfall buckets or snake traps (Corn 1994; Enge 2001; Fisher & Case 2000a, b; Fitch 1992; Greenberg et al. 1994). Ground cover boards are placed near one arm of each array in the PLECA specifically to sample California legless lizards (*Anniella pulchra*) and smaller snakes such as the ring-necked snake (*Diadophis punctatus*) and night snake (*Hypsiglena torquata*).

During each week of sampling, ambient temperature was recorded for 5 of the 20 pitfall arrays in SAMO and 3 of the 16 pitfall arrays at CABR using HOBO gauges (Onset, Inc.). HOBO gauges were hung approximately 0.5 meters off the ground from a wooden stake. A 5-gallon white

3

plastic bucket was placed upside down over the wooden stake to protect the HOBOs from rain and direct sunlight.

Amphibian and reptile monitoring at CHIS uses cover board trapping rather than pitfall trapping (Feller et al. 1988). All four transects surveyed in 2009 included a total of 60 cover boards arranged in two rows of 30. The rows were approximately 5 meters apart and the spacing between boards was approximately 5 meters. The boards were 12 in. x 12 in. x 2 in. pieces of Douglas Fir (*Pseudotsuga menziesii*) lumber, and each board was consecutively numbered from 1 to 60 on the underside with a black permanent ink marker. Boards were placed in contact with smooth, mineral soil. When the boards were turned over, any animals present were captured, identified, measured, and released. Animals that escape without being captured were included in the abundance index, but their data was excluded from the analysis of body length. Body length was measured from the tip of the snout to the opening of the vent (snout-vent length, SVL). Lizards are not marked, therefore re-captures are not identifiable.

As described in the legacy protocol for CHIS (Fellers et al. 1988), a population index value was calculated for each species for each transect by combining the data for each sampling period and calculating the capture rate as the number of animals of each species detected (including animals which escaped before handling) by the total number of boards that were checked in a transect. All transects surveyed in 2009 had 60 cover boards. For example, if there are 60 boards, and spring numbers = x, and fall numbers = y, then the annual index = x + y/120.

The CHIS monitoring protocol also calls for a calculation of weight-length regressions. The mass of an animal relative to its length can provide an indication of its health, because healthier animals of a given length are likely to weigh more.

Site Selection and Sampling Frequency

Santa Monica Mountains National Recreation Area

The monitoring protocol (Busteed et al. 2006) identified five sampling regions in the greater Santa Monica Mountains (SMM) ecosystem (Simi Hills, Western SMM, Central SMM, Malibu Creek Watershed, and Eastern SMM). Pitfall-trapping sites were distributed across habitat types and areas with varying degrees of urban impact using judgment sampling. Several factors governed the placement of trap arrays: vegetation, terrain, proximity to trails, proximity to archaeological sites, and ease of accessibility. Suitable trap array sites were selected after examination of topographic maps and site visits.

Data collection (pitfall trapping) in SAMO follows a rotating panel design on a by-region basis. During 2009, monitoring was carried out in one sampling region, the southern portion of the Malibu Creek watershed area. The Malibu Creek watershed is the second largest discrete watershed draining into the Santa Monica Bay, and is in the heart of the Santa Monica Mountains (Figure 1).

There were 20 pitfall arrays monitored (Figure 2A and 2B) in this area during 2009. Different vegetation types were associated with arrays, with the majority of them being in grassland or woodland habitats (Table 1).

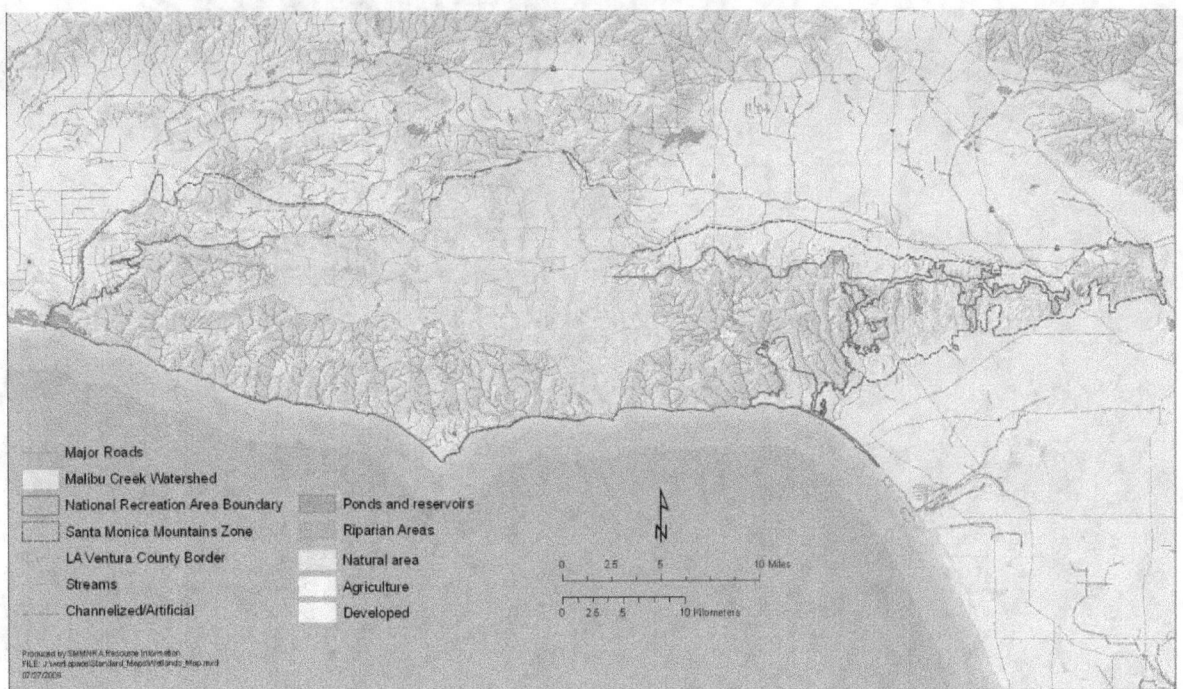

Figure 1. The Malibu Creek watershed area (yellow) in Santa Monica Mountains National Recreation Area and Simi Hills.

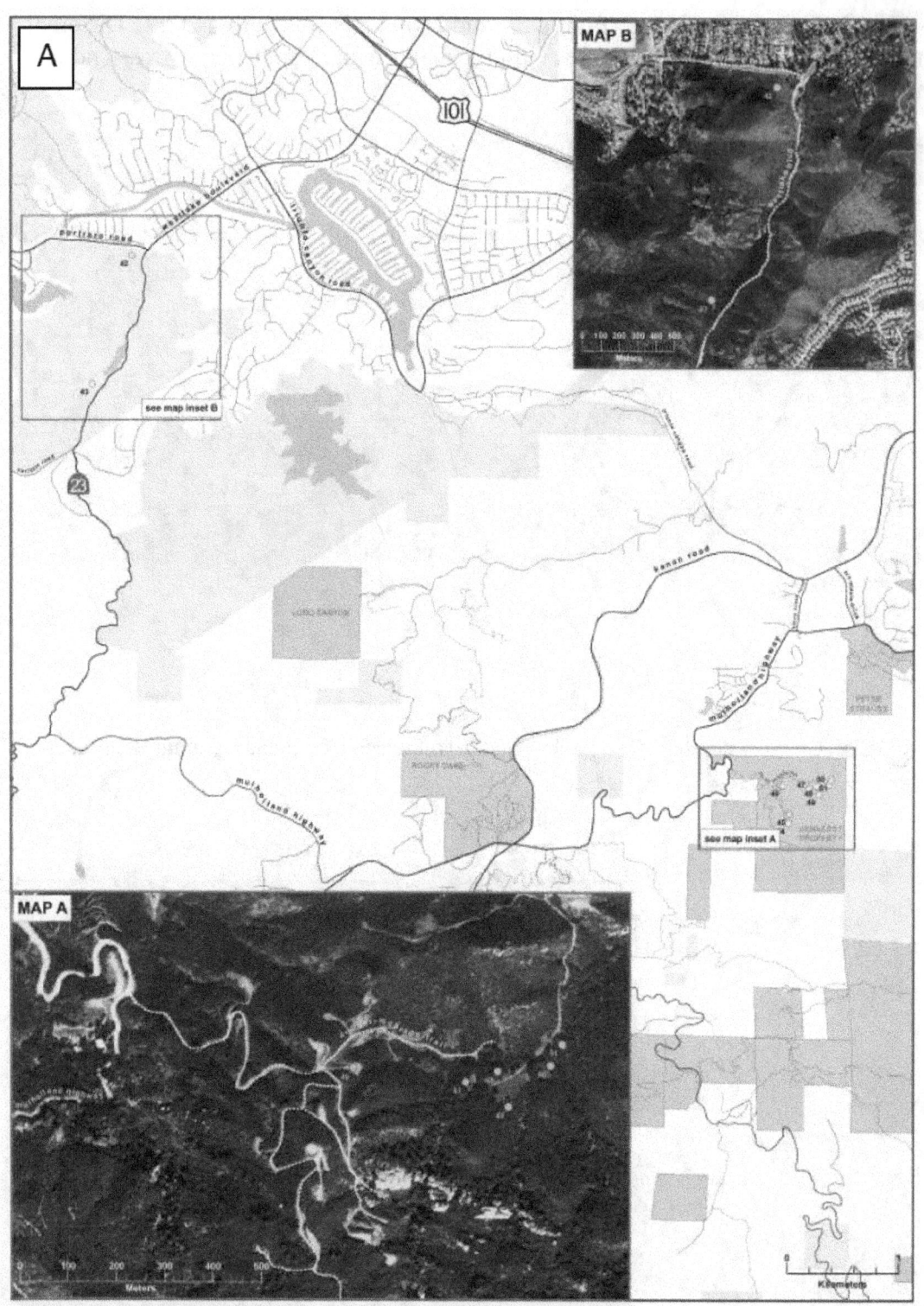

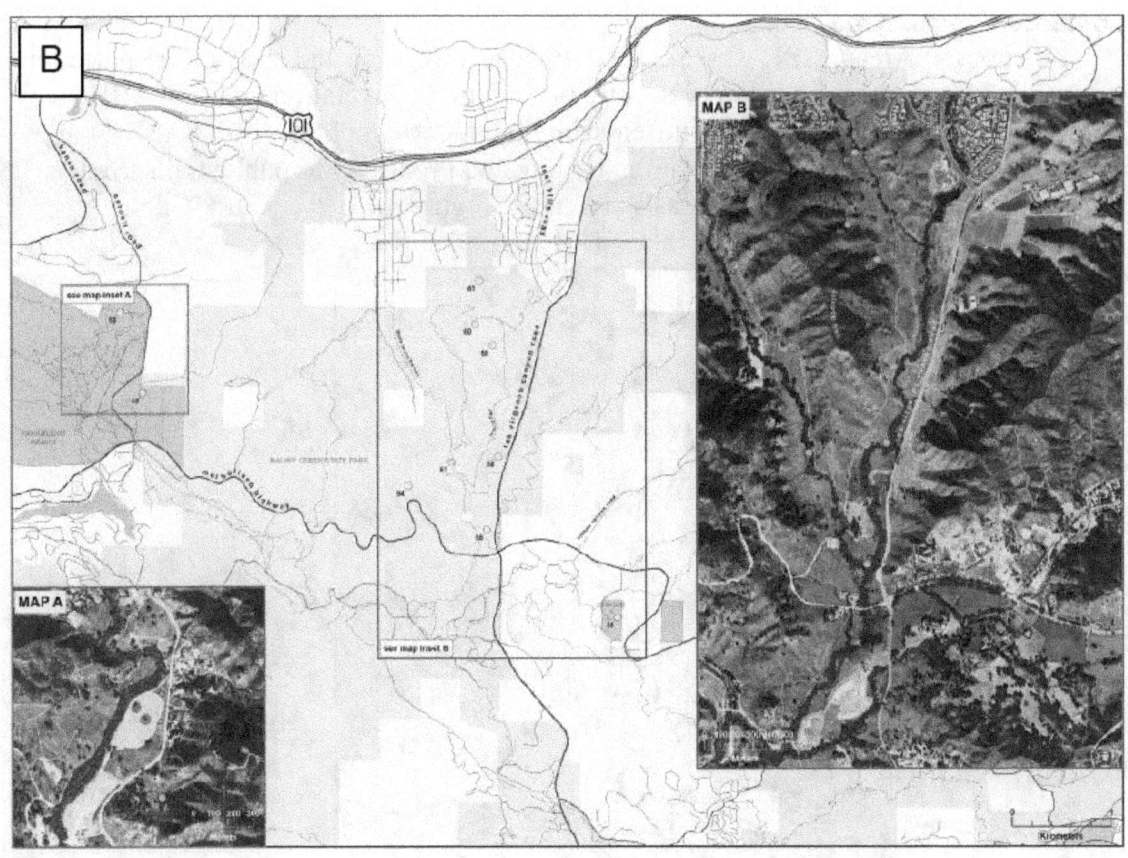

Figure 2. Maps of pitfall traps monitored in the Malibu watershed area of SMMNRA in 2009. Map insets are aerial photographs shown for detail. A) Arrays 42-51, B) Arrays 52-61.

Table 1. The general vegetation type associated with each of the 20 pitfall arrays in Santa Monica Mountains National Recreation Area.

Array Number	Vegetation	Array Number	Vegetation
42	Grass	52	Grass
43	Coastal Sage Scrub	53	Woodland
44	Chaparral	54	Grass
45	Chaparral	55	Woodland
46	Grass	56	Grass
47	Woodland	57	Woodland
48	Woodland	58	Grass
49	Chaparral	59	Woodland
50	Woodland	60	Woodland
51	Woodland	61	Grass

Point Loma Ecological Area

Point Loma Ecological Area/CABR was stratified by vegetation type and arrays were placed in each stratum in approximate proportion to the proportion of that vegetation type at CABR. Specific sites for pitfall trap arrays were chosen using judgment sampling. As in SAMO, the location of arrays was influenced by vegetation, terrain, and proximity to public trails. Sixteen pitfall arrays are monitored on an annual basis at CABR (Figure 3).

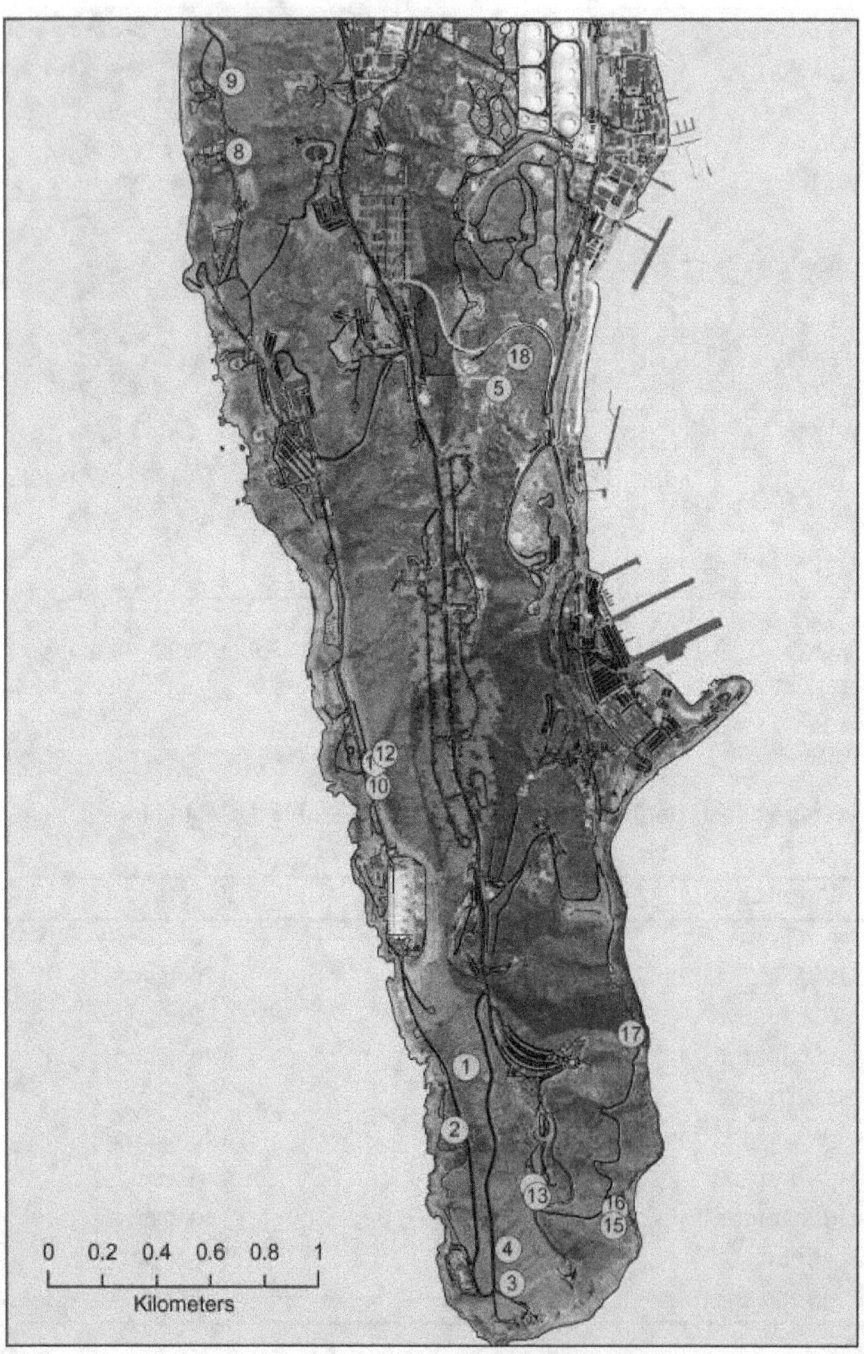

Figure 3. Maps of pitfall traps monitored at CABR in 2009.

8

Channel Islands National Park

As described in Fellers et al. (1988) specific sites for cover board transects at CHIS were selected using judgment sampling (Figures 4 and 5). In 2009, sampling at CHIS was conducted on one transect on Santa Barbara Island (Figure 4), and on three transects on San Miguel Island, (Figure 5).

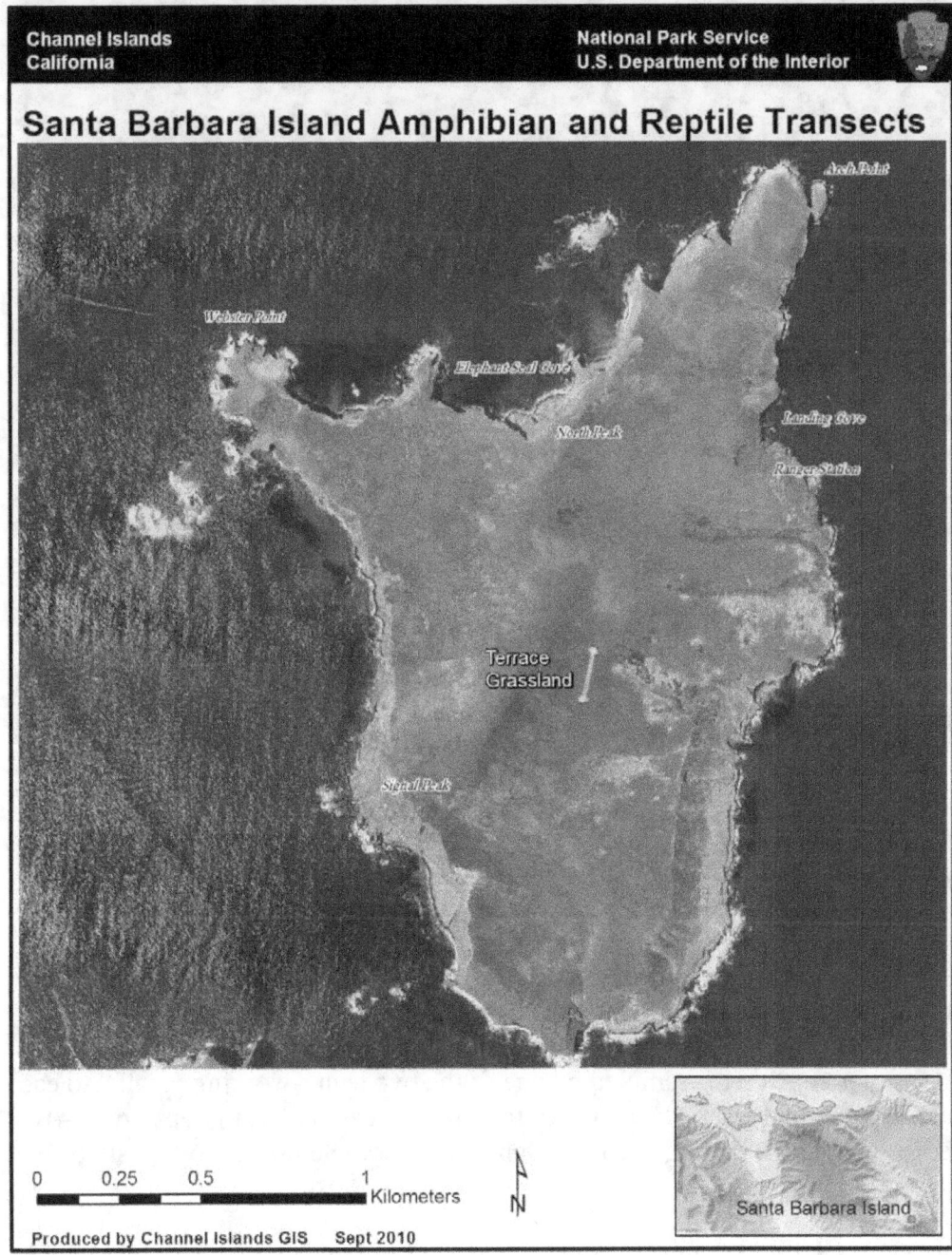

Figure 4. Location of the cover board transect in terrace grassland habitat on Santa Barbara Island, California.

Figure 5. Amphibian and reptile cover board transects on San Miguel Island, California. Fellers et al. (1988) describe the location of each transects according to the names shown on the map.

Frequency and Timing of Sampling

At both SAMO and CABR, each pitfall array was sampled for four consecutive days, typically Monday (when the traps were opened) through Friday (when the traps were closed) once a month from February through December in 2009. Each sampling event includes visiting all pitfall trap arrays subject to sampling that year. Examination of pitfall traps is labor intensive, and it is important that all sites be visited in a relatively short period of time in order to reduce the mortality from overheating of incidentally captured small mammals. Arrays at SAMO are organized into sets of two. Each set is sampled by one of the two teams working parallel to each other. Concurrent sampling minimizes the length of time specimens are left in traps. At CABR arrays are sampled sequentially by a single team which usually completes the work in six or seven hours per day.

Each of the 4 transects at CHIS was sampled at least twice a year, once in the spring and the fall. Additional surveys were conducted on a monthly basis between December and May when sufficient personnel were available.

Results

Santa Monica Mountains National Recreation Area

Sampling
Because of cold temperatures and a markedly decreased capture rate, we did not monitor arrays in January 2009. Arrays in all other months were monitored for a total of 11 trap months. This yielded a total of 43 trap days in 2009. There were 12 observers performing pitfall trapping during 2009.

Temperature
Temperatures varied widely in SAMO from February to December 2009 (Figure 6). The maximum temperature recorded (120°F) was recorded in June, and the minimum temperature (20°F) was recorded in November.

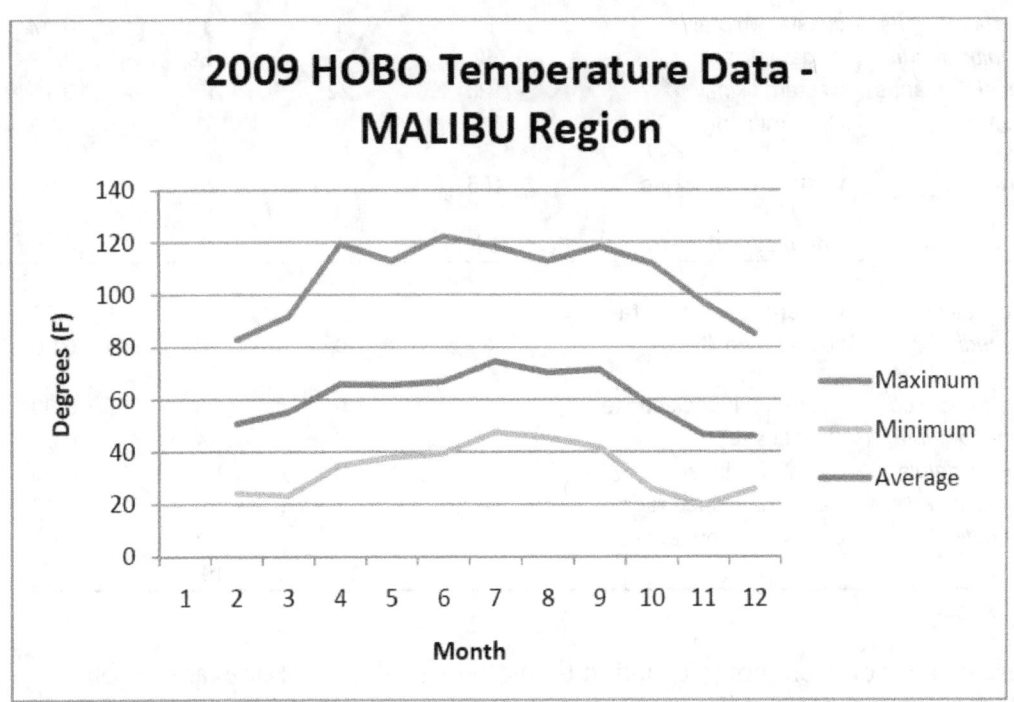

Figure 6. The average, highest and lowest temperatures recorded during each month in 2009 in the Malibu Creek watershed. Average monthly temperatures were calculated using temperature data from all HOBO gauges (*N*=5).

Captures and Re-captures
In SAMO, we captured individuals from 17 different reptile and amphibian species within the Malibu Creek Watershed in 2009 (Table 2; 4 amphibian species, 6 lizard species, and 7 snake species). Trapping at the pitfall arrays (including snake traps) in 2009 yielded a total of 30 snake captures, 402 lizard captures, and 429 amphibian captures. In 2009, we also had 1 snake re-capture, 111 lizard re-captures, and 27 amphibian re-captures (Table 2). The proportion of individuals re-captured varied among species. However, some species like *Batrachyseps nigrivensis* were not toe-clipped, because of their small size, which makes identifying re-captures difficult. Batrachyseps could only be identified as recaptures if they had been initially captured

11

and a tail sample was taken within the sampling week. Western fence lizards had the highest proportion of re-captures (29%).

Table 2: The number of individual captures, re-captures, and the proportion re-captured for each species sampled in the Malibu Creek Watershed within Santa Monica Mountains National Recreation Area in 2009.

Species Code	Species	Common Name	Individual captures	Re-captures	Total captures	Proportion re-captured
Amphibians						
BANI	*Batrachyseps nigrivensis*	black-bellied slender salamander	409	26	435	0.06
BUBO	*Bufo boreas*	western toad	11	1	12	0.08
ENES	*Ensatina eschscholtzii*	Monterey ensatina	2	0	2	0.00
HYRE	*Hyla regilla*	Pacific treefrog	7	0	7	0.00
Lizards						
CNTI	*Cnemidophorus tigris*	coastal whiptail	14	1	15	0.07
ELMU	*Elgaria multicarinata*	Alligator lizard	52	7	59	0.12
EUSK	*Eumeces skiltonianus*	western skink	128	22	150	0.15
PHCO	*Phrynosoma coronatum*	California horned lizard	1	0	1	0.00
SCOC	*Sceloporus occidentalis*	western fence lizard	186	77	263	0.29
UTST	*Uta stansburiana*	side-blotched lizard	21	4	25	0.16
Snakes						
COCO	*Coluber constrictor*	western yellowbelly racer	3	0	3	0.00
CRVI	*Crotalus viridis*	southern pacific rattlesnake	3	0	3	0.00
DIPU	*Diadophis punctatus*	western ringneck snake	8	0	8	0.00
HYTO	*Hypsiglena torquata*	night snake	4	0	4	0.00
LAGE	*Lampropeltis getula*	California kingsnake	1	0	1	0.00
MALA	*Masticophis lateralis*	California striped racer	7	1	8	0.13
PICA	*Pituophis catenifer*	San Diego gopher snake	4	0	4	0.00
TOTAL			861	139	1000	

Some species were much more commonly captured than others (Table 3). For example, black-bellied salamanders represented almost half (47%) of the total captures in 2009. Ten out of 17 species comprised less than 1% of the total animals caught. The number of captures per species varied by array (Figures 7-9). There were 15 out of 20 pitfall arrays where we captured at least one snake in 2009 (Figure 9).

Table 3: The percentage of total captures by species in the Malibu Creek Watershed within Santa Monica Mountains National Recreation Area.

Species Code	Percent of all captures
BANI	47.50
BUBO	1.28
CNTI	1.63
COCO	0.35
CRVI	0.35
DIPU	0.93
ELMU	6.04
ENES	0.23
EUSK	14.87
HYRE	0.81
HYTO	0.46
LAGE	0.12
MALA	0.81
PHCO	0.12
PICA	0.46
SCOC	21.60
UTST	2.44
TOTAL	100

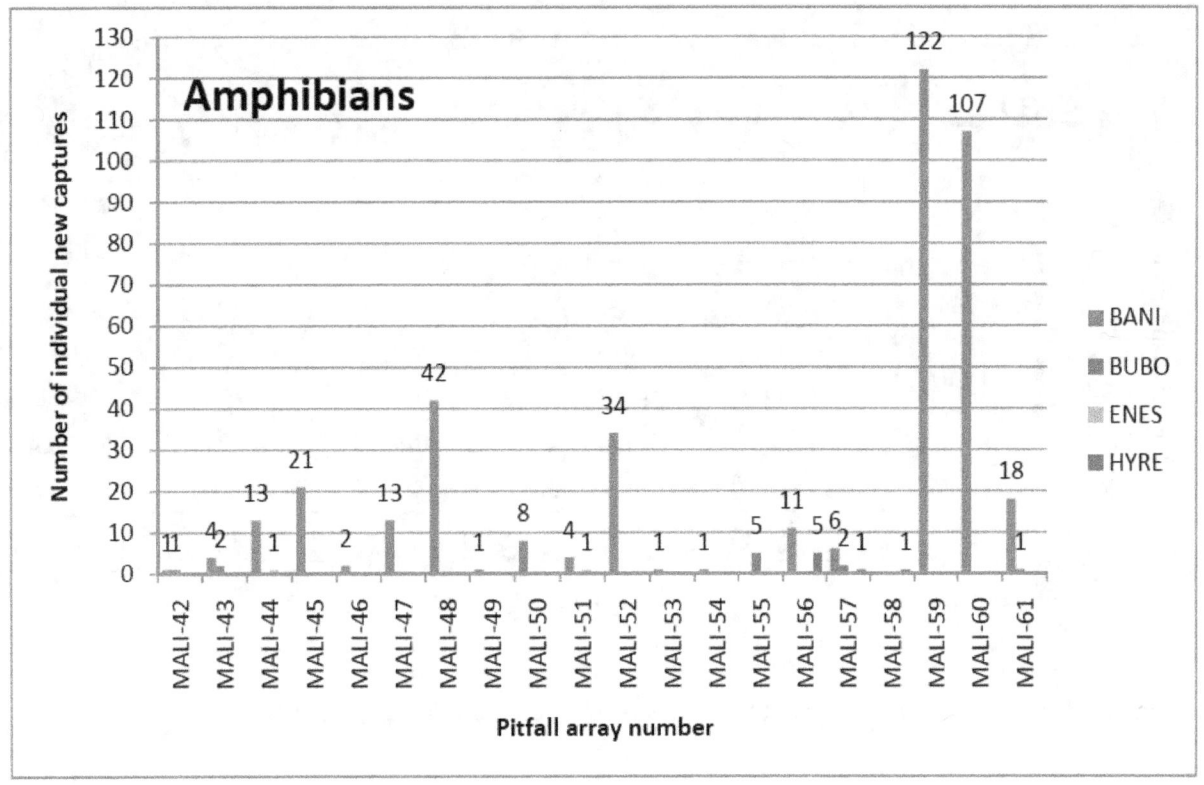

Figure 7. The number of individual captures (excluding re-captures) of amphibians by array.

13

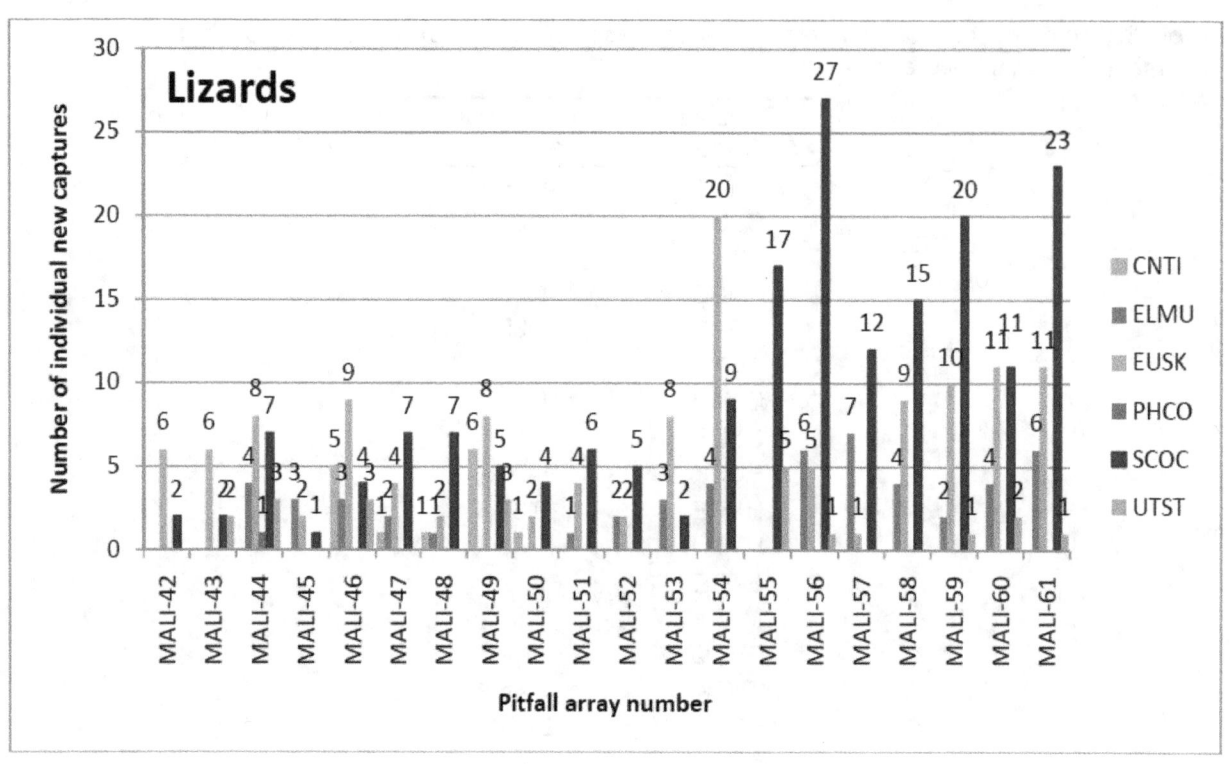

Figure 8. The number of individual captures (excluding re-captures) for lizards by array.

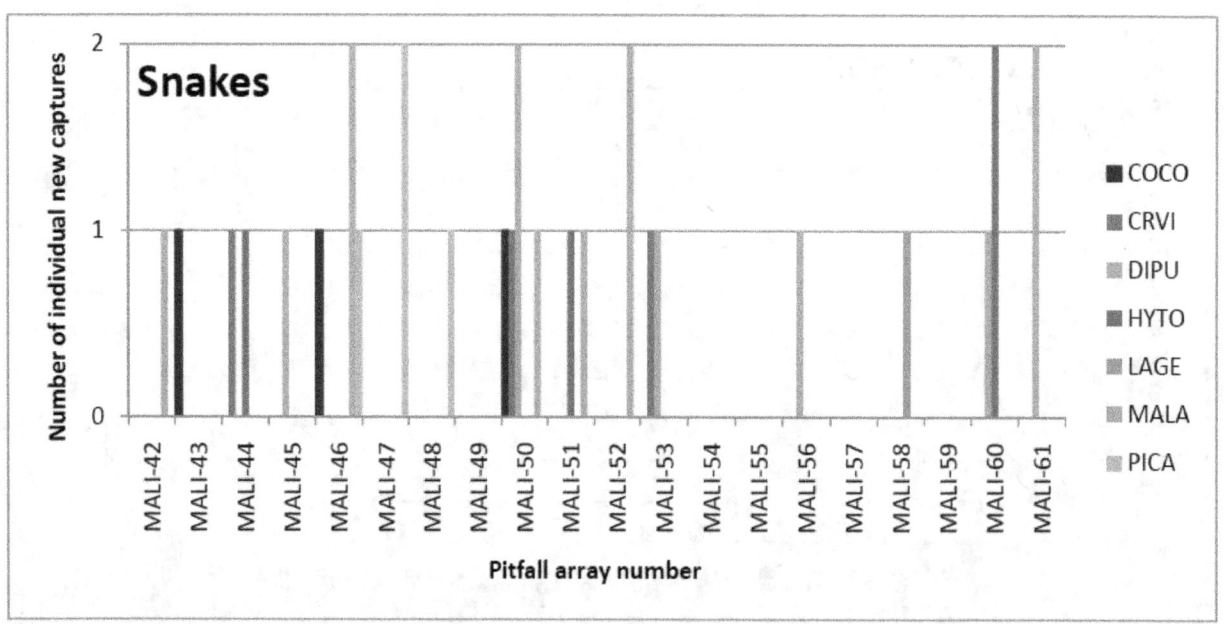

Figure 9. The number of individual captures (excluding recaptures) for snakes by array.

Captures by month

There were more amphibian captures during the winter and spring in 2009, which corresponded to the wettest time of the year in SAMO (Table 4). In contrast, lizards and snakes were more often captured during the driest and hottest months during the summer and fall.

Table 4. The total number of individuals captured and the number of different species captured by month.

Species Code	Feb.	Mar	Apr	May	Jun	Jul	Aug	Sep	Oct	Nov	Dec
Amphibians											
BANI	56	11	75	7	0	0	0	0	135	6	119
BUBO	0	0	6	1	2	0	1	0	1	0	0
ENES	0	0	2	0	0	0	0	0	0	0	0
HYRE	4	1	0	0	0	0	0	0	1	0	1
Lizards											
CNTI	0	0	0	1	1	6	1	5	0	0	0
ELMU	2	4	18	6	5	5	6	4	2	0	0
EUSK	1	24	4	2	15	47	22	12	1	0	0
PHCO	0	0	0	0	0	0	1	0	0	0	0
SCOC	6	24	19	22	17	26	36	14	14	8	0
UTST	0	1	1	0	0	10	5	3	1	0	0
Snakes											
COCO	0	0	1	1	0	1	0	0	0	0	0
CRVI	0	0	0	1	1	0	0	0	1	0	0
DIPU	0	0	5	0	0	0	1	1	1	0	0
HYTO	0	0	1	0	2	0	1	0	0	0	0
LAGE	0	0	0	0	0	0	0	1	0	0	0
MALA	0	2	1	0	1	0	0	3	0	0	0
PICA	0	1	1	0	1	0	1	0	0	0	0
Total individuals	69	68	134	41	45	95	75	43	157	14	120
Number of species	6	8	12	8	9	6	10	8	9	2	2

Captures by Habitat Type

The number of amphibians, lizards, and snakes captured varied by habitat type (Figures 10-12). We caught the highest number of black-bellied slender salamanders at two of the oak woodland sites (Array 59 and 60, Figure 10). Grassland and some of the oak woodland sites captured the highest number of individual lizards (Figure 11).

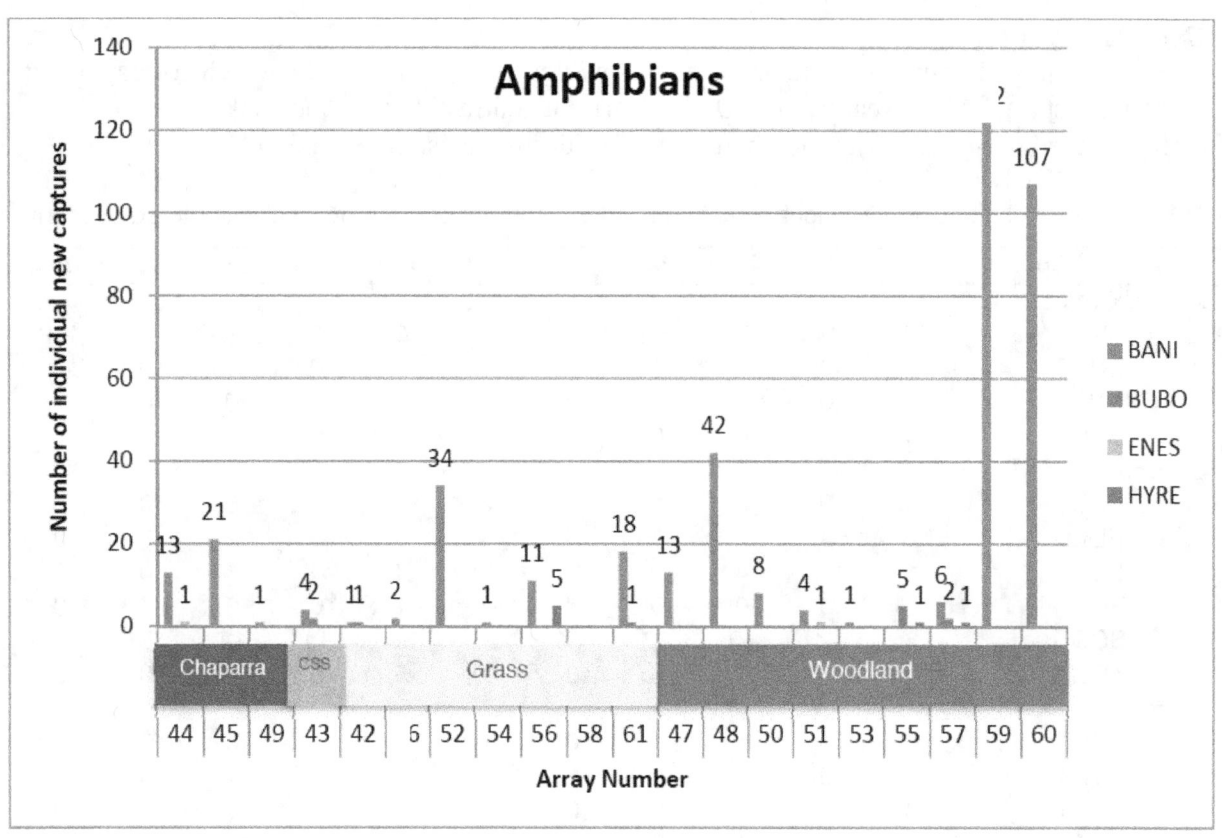

Figure 10.   r   of amphibians by habitat types   a   coastal sage scrub, grass, and woodland) in the l   l   u   t   e   w   t   n   tains National Recreation Area during 2009.

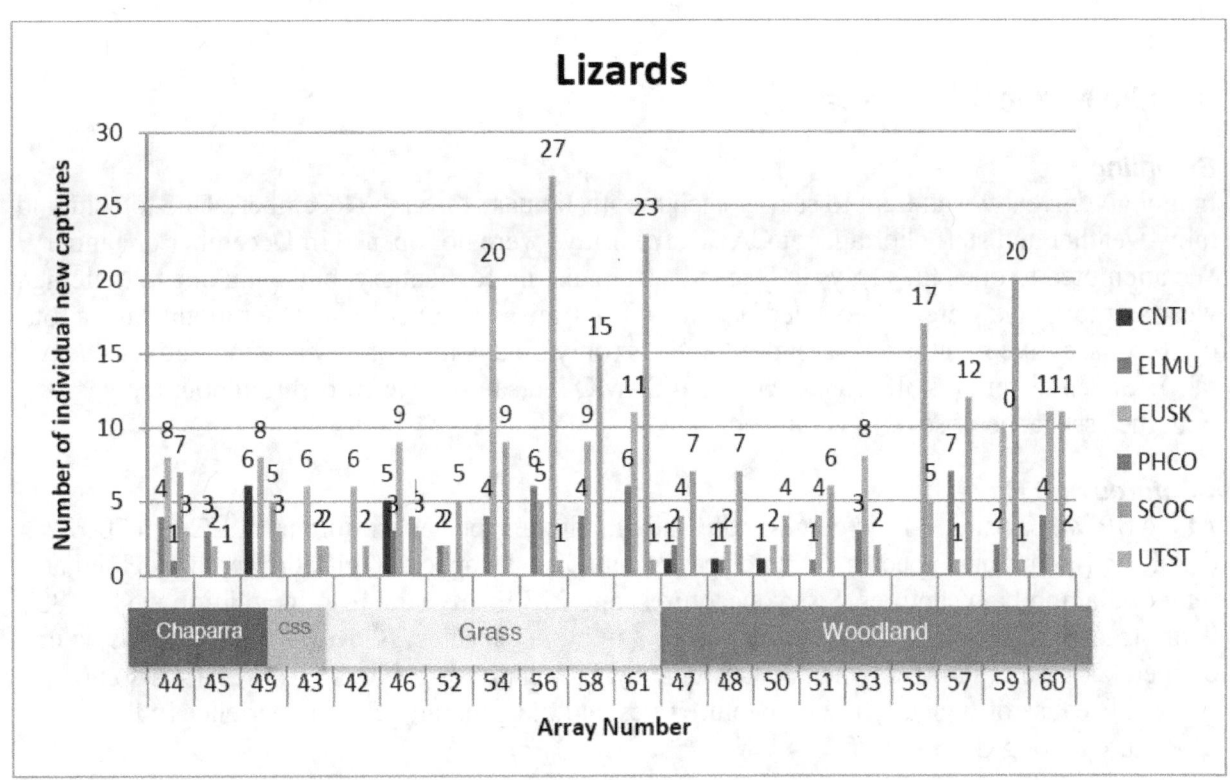

Figure 11. Individual new capts of lizards by habitat type in the Mabeshed within Santa iie tion Area during 2009.

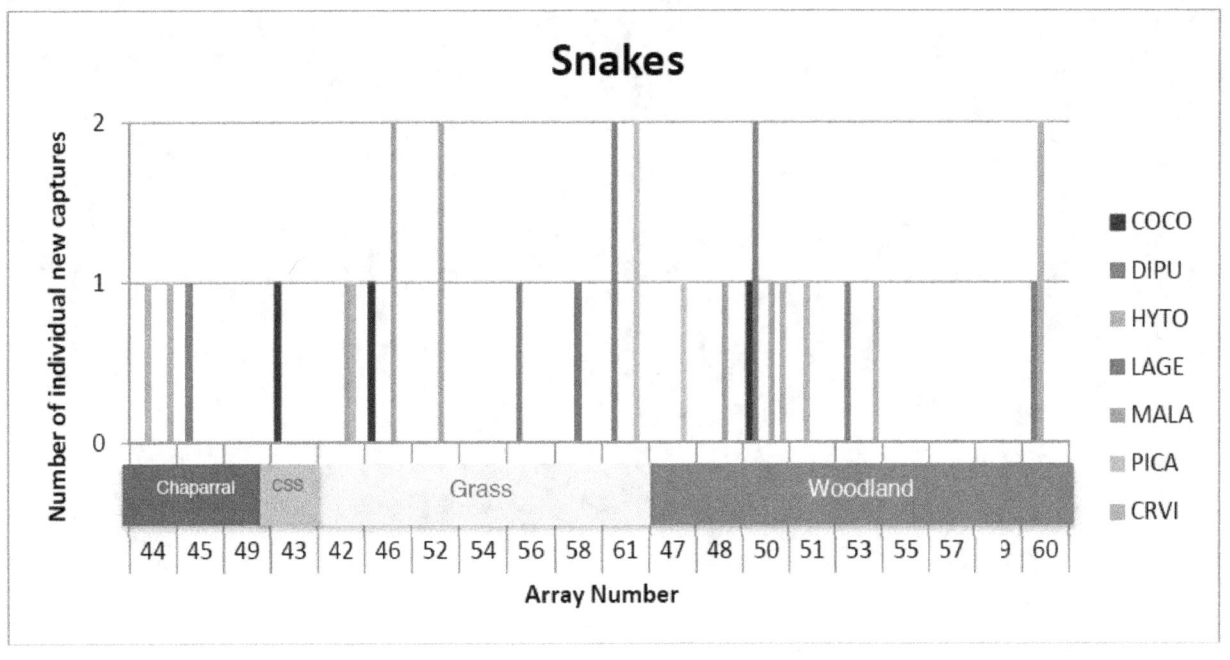

Figure 12. Individual new caps of snakes by habitat type in thshed within Santa Monica Mountainsie tion Area during 2009.

Cabrillo National Monument

Sampling

In any given year we attempt to survey each month January through December. Due to cold and rainy weather and staff shortages at CABR, the arrays were not opened in December or January. We attempted to open the arrays in December to make up for January, but again due to inclement weather the arrays were only opened one day. The traps were opened all other months for a total of 10 consecutive months and a total of 40 days (only 3 days in February due to relatively heavy rain). Seven different staff from CABR and SAMO led sampling efforts throughout the year with the assistance of several volunteers.

Captures and Re-captures

At CABR we captured 11 different reptile and amphibian species within the PLECA in 2009 (Table 6: 1 amphibian species, 5 lizard species and 5 snake species). Pitfall trapping yielded a total of 3 amphibian captures, 8 snake captures, and 273 lizard captures. In addition we had 88 lizard re-captures. At CABR our only known amphibian species, *Batrachoceps pacificus*, is not clipped because of its size, which makes identifying recaptures difficult. Snakes are also not marked because of typically low re-capture rates and the general lack of experience in the procedure among CABR staff.

Table 5: The number of individual captures, recaptures, and the proportion recaptured for each species sampled in 2009 in CABR.

Species Code	Species	Common Name	Individual captures	Re-captures	Total captures	Proportion Re-captured
Amphibians						
BAPA	*Batrachoseps pacificus*	Pacific slender salamander	3	0	3	0.00
Lizards						
ANPU	*Anniella pulchra*	Legless Lizard	2	0	2	0.00
CNHY	*Cnemidophorus hyperythrus*	Orange-throated whiptail	60	20	80	0.25
ELMU	*Elgaria multicarinata*	San Diego alligator lizard	24	7	31	0.23
SCOC	*Sceloporus occidentalis*	Great Basin fence lizard	99	29	128	0.23
UTST	*Uta stansburiana*	California side-blotched lizard	88	32	120	0.27
Snakes						
CRVI	*Crotalus viridis*	Southern Pacific rattlesnake	2	0	2	0.00
DIPU	*Diadophis punctatus*	Western ringneck snake	1	0	1	0.00
LAGE	*Lampropeltis getula*	California kingsnake	1	0	1	0.00
MALA	*Masticophis lateralis*	California striped racer	3	0	3	0.00
PIME	*Pituophis melanoleucas*	Gopher snake	1	0	1	0.00
TOTAL			284	88	372	

For each of the four most common lizards encountered at CABR (from most to least captured; SCOC, UTST, CNHY, and ELMU) approximately one quarter of the total respective captures were re-captures (Table 5: 23-27%).

Western fence lizards (SCOC) and side-blotched lizards (UTST) were the two most common species captured and were caught in roughly equal numbers (128 SCOC and 120 UTST). Together they represent 67% of all captures. The orange-throated whiptail (CNHY) was the next most common (80 captures and 22% of all captures) followed by alligator lizards (ELMU; 31 captures and 8% of all captures). Anecdotal observations from CABR support these proportions. Snakes are not marked at CABR but it should be noted that *Crotalus viridis*, *Diadophis punctatus*, *Lampropeltis getula* and *Pituophis melanoleucas* were observed regularly around CABR suggesting their populations are greater than might be concluded from the array data. A legless lizard (ANPU) was observed at least once in the breezeway of the CABR visitor center during 2009, which is some distance from Array Loma-09 where this species was captured. This observation suggests ANPU is not limited to just the area around Array Loma-09.

Captures by Array

Only three individual amphibians (*Batrachoceps pacificus*) were caught in two arrays (Loma-11 and Loma-16; Figure 13.). However, Loma-11 is located on Navy Base Point Loma on the west side of the peninsula and further north in the PLECA than CABR proper. Loma-16 is located on the eastern side of the peninsula within CABR (Figure 3). These captures suggest that *Batrachoceps pacificus* may be distributed along the length of both sides of the peninsula.

The capture rate of lizards was variable among all arrays (Figure 14). Western fence lizards (SCOC) and side-blotched lizards (UTST) were captured in all arrays except Loma-8 which did not catch any UTST. Orange-throated whiptails (CNHY) were caught at least once, and sometimes often, at every array except Loma-11 and Loma-18. Alligator lizards (ELMU) were not captured at arrays Loma-2, Loma-14, Loma-15, and Loma-18, but otherwise were captured relatively evenly between arrays. No arrays stand out as capturing significantly more or significantly less of any lizard species or total lizards.

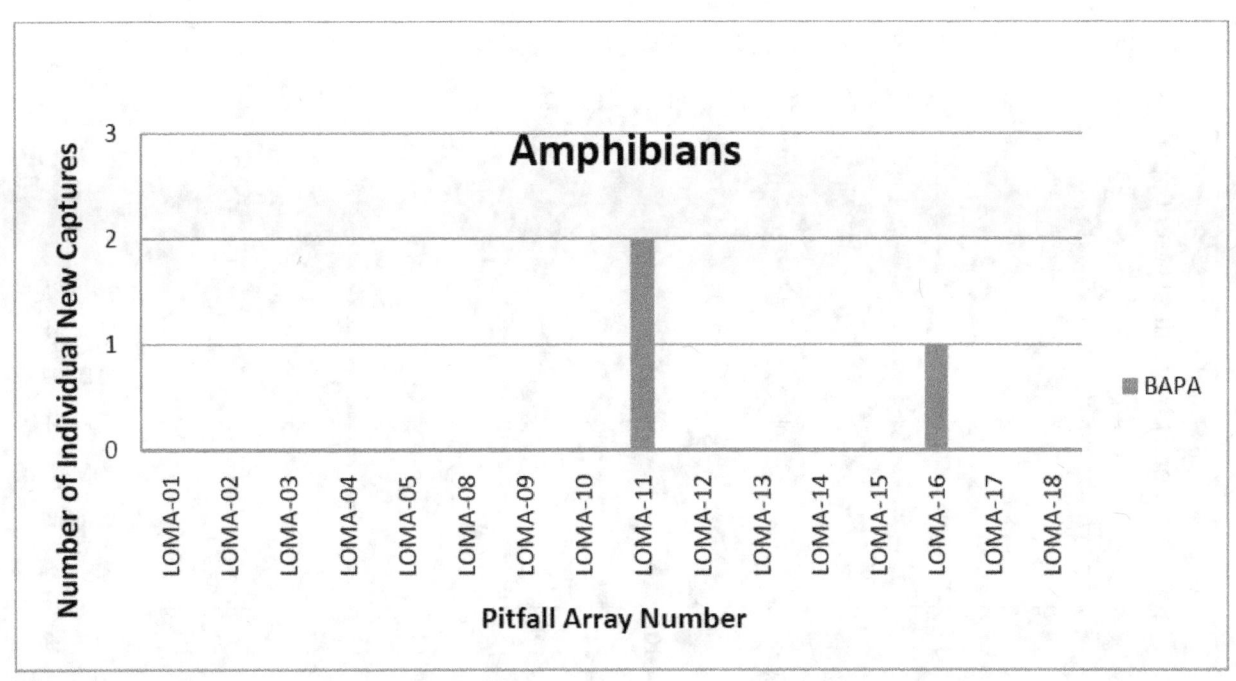

Figure 13. The number of individual captures (not re-captures) of amphibians by array at CABR during 2009.

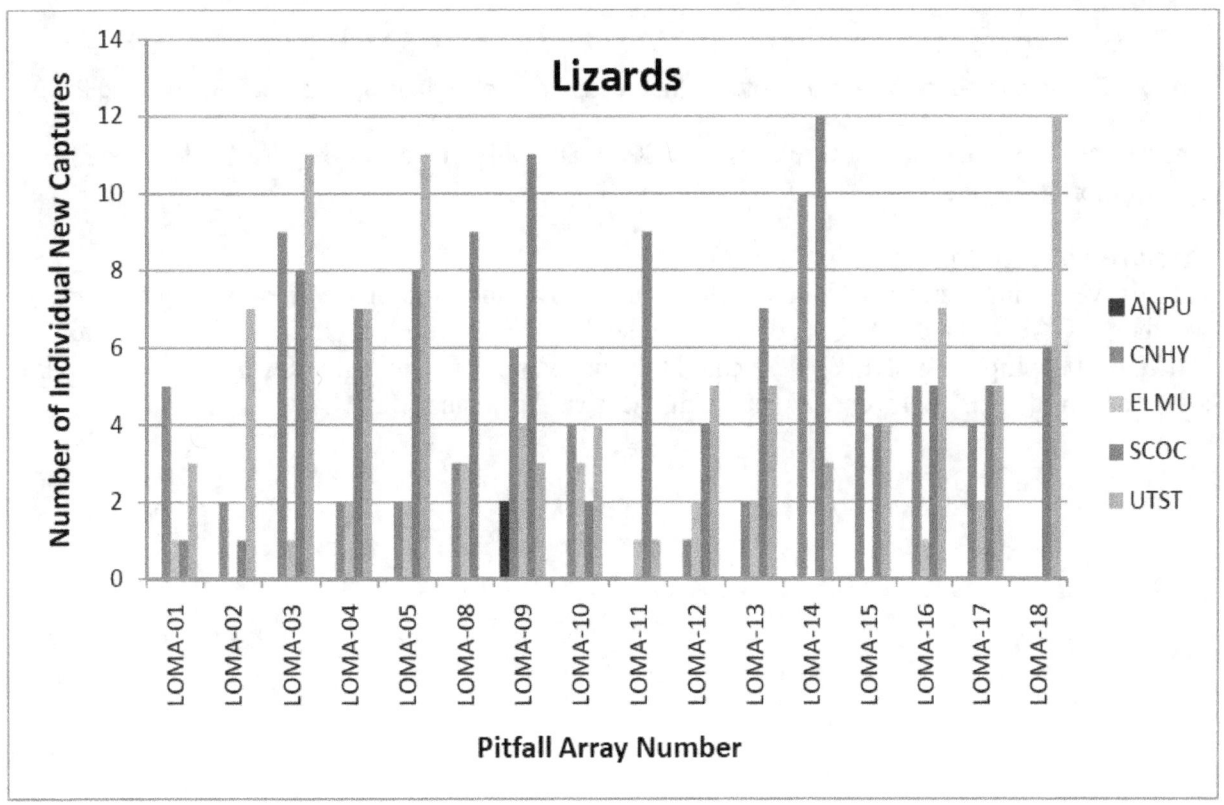

Figure 14. The number of individual captures (not re-captures) of lizards by array at CABR.

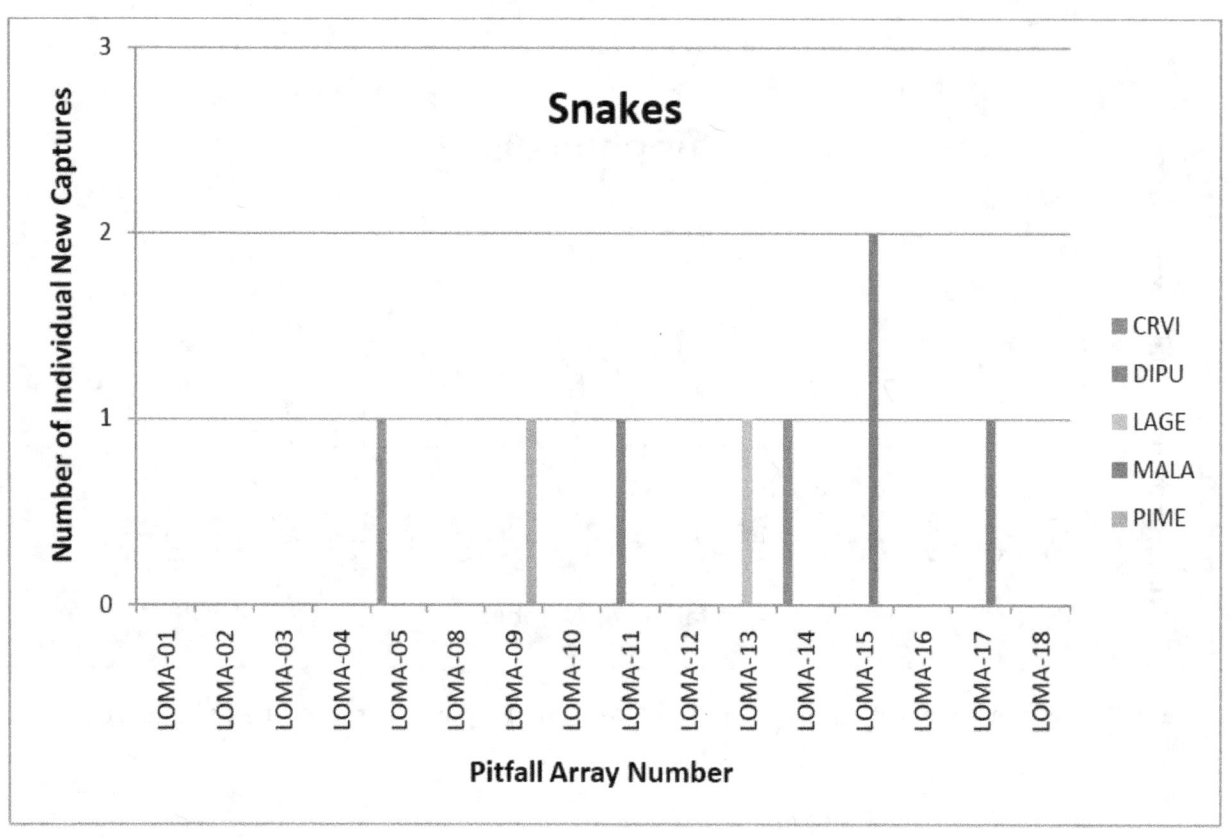

Figure 15. The number of individual captures (not recaptures) of snakes by array at CABR during 2009.

Only eight individual snakes were caught in 2009, and only one array (Figure 15, Loma-15) caught more than one.

Captures by Month

Lizards were caught steadily from March through November, roughly corresponding to milder weather at CABR (Table 6). Five of the eight snakes (63%) were caught in April. Over half (56%) of the whiptails (CNHY) were caught during May, June and July. Over half (58%) of the alligator lizards (ELMU) were caught during March, April, and May.

Table 6. The total number of individuals captured and the number of different species captured by month at CABR.

Species Code	Feb	Mar	Apr	May	Jun	Jul	Aug	Sep	Oct	Nov	Dec
Amphibians											
BAPA	3	0	0	0	0	0	0	0	0	0	0
Lizards											
ANPU	0	0	0	2	0	0	0	0	0	0	0
CNHY	0	3	5	16	16	13	7	6	6	8	0
ELMU	2	8	4	6	1	3	3	1	2	1	0
SCOC	13	23	17	12	14	12	9	7	11	10	0
UTST	7	8	14	10	7	10	7	16	20	17	4
Snakes											
CRVI	0	0	1	0	0	1	0	0	0	0	0
DIPU	0	0	1	0	0	0	0	0	0	0	0
LAGE	0	0	0	0	0	1	0	0	0	0	0
MALA	0	0	2	0	1	0	0	0	0	0	0
PIME	0	0	1	0	0	0	0	0	0	0	0
Total Individuals	22	42	45	46	39	40	26	30	39	36	4
Number of Species	4	4	8	5	5	6	4	4	4	4	1

Channel Islands National Park

A total of 73 individual animals belonging to three lizard species and one salamander species were observed during ten surveys conducted between January and December 2009. Each transect was surveyed at least twice during this time period and population indices are provided in Table 7. On Santa Barbara Island, 18 island night lizards were captured (Table 7). On San Miguel Island, 39 slender salamanders, 13 alligator lizards, and 3 fence lizards were captured (Table 7). The population index is simply the number of individuals observed divided by the number of cover boards. For each species, we compared each individual's weight with its snout-vent length with linear regression (Figures 3-6).

Table 7. The 2009 population index values calculated for the total number of each amphibian and reptile species detected under cover boards tabulated by island, transect, and survey date. SBI-TG = Santa Barbara Island, Terrace Grassland, SMI-AS = San Miguel Island, Air Strip, SMI-NI = San Miguel Island, Nidever Canyon, SMI-WC = San Miguel Island, Willow Canyon. XR = *Xantusia riversiana* = Island night lizard, BP = *Batrachoseps pacificus* = Channel Islands slender salamander, EM = *Elgaria multicarinata* = Southern alligator lizard, SO = *Sceloporus occidentalis becki* = Island fence lizard.

Island-Transect	Survey Date	Species Code	Total # Animals	Total # Boards	Population Index Value
SB-TG	3/14/2009	XR	13	60	
	10/24/2009	XR	5	60	0.150
SM-AS	2/4/2009	BP	4	60	
	12/12/2009	BP	16	60	0.167
SM-NC	2/22/2009	BP	7	60	
	12/13/2009	BP	10	60	0.142
SM-WC	1/23/2009	BP	1	60	
	5/11/2009	BP	1	60	0.017
SM-AS	2/4/2009	EM	2*	60	
	4/18/2009	EM	1	60	
	12/12/2009	EM	2	60	0.028
SM-WC	1/23/2009	EM	2	60	
	5/11/2009	EM	1	60	
	12/22/2009	EM	5	60	0.044
SM-AS	4/18/2009	SO	1	60	
	12/12/2009	SO	1	60	0.017
SM-WC	5/11/2009	SO	1	60	0.017

*One animal escaped before being handled. Escaped animals are used as part of the population index calculation, but not for the weight-length regressions.

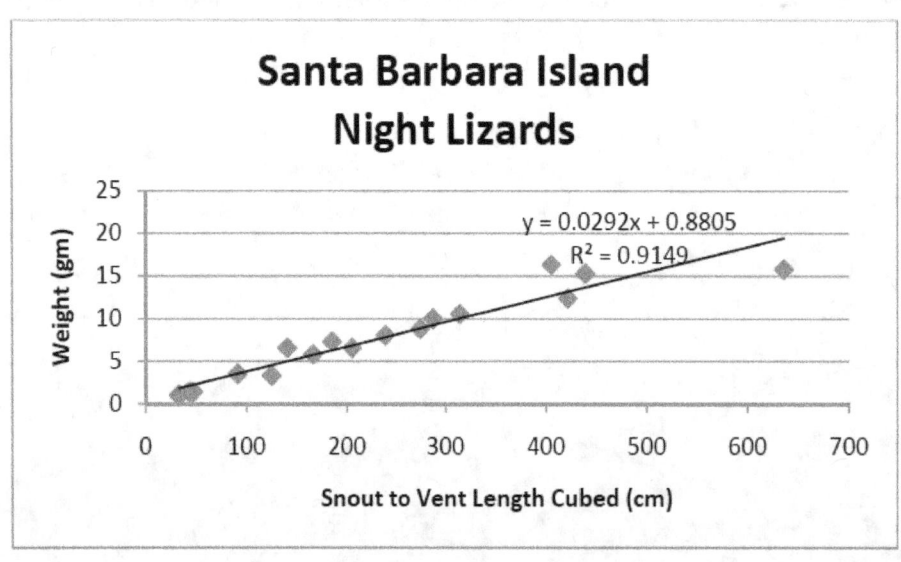

Figure 16. Santa Barbara Island night lizard weight-length regression, 2009.

24

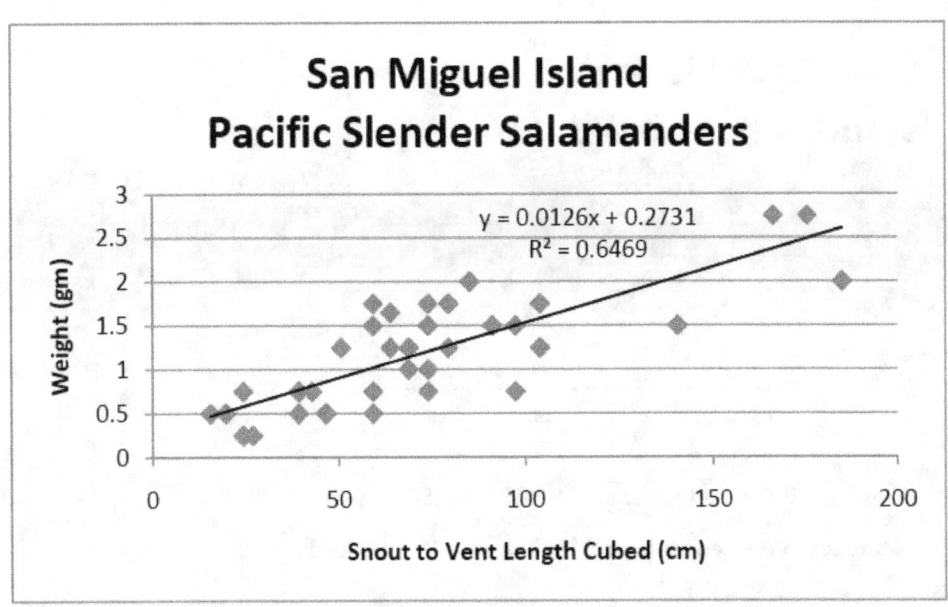

Figure 17. The 2009 weight-length regression for the Channel Island slender salamander on San Miguel Island.

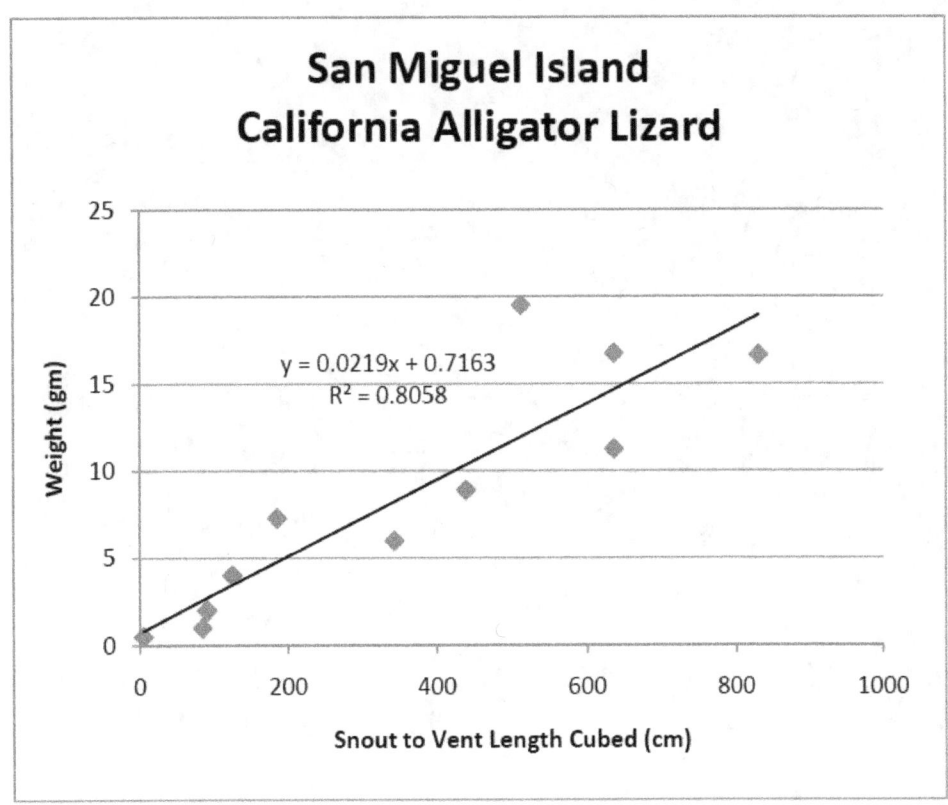

Figure 18. The 2009 weight-length regression for the California alligator lizard on San Miguel Island.

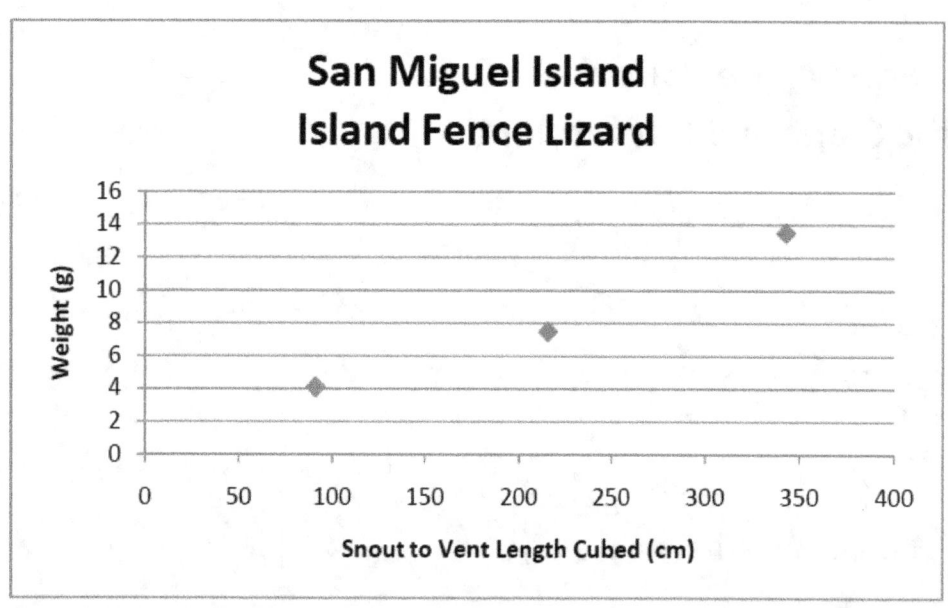

Figure 19. The 2009 weight-length data for the island fence lizard on San Miguel Island.

Discussion

Santa Monica Mountains National Recreation Area

Lizards and amphibians were caught more often than snakes. However, the diversity of species captured was greater for snakes than any other group. The most commonly captured species was the black-bellied slender salamander (BANI), which were 95% of our total amphibian captures, and 47% of our total captures in 2009 (Table 2). These small salamanders are actively moving during rainy nights, and we have captured up to 84 individuals in a single morning during the wet winter and spring months. The most common lizard species captured were western fence lizard and western skink. Together, these two species were 78% of all lizard captures in 2009 (Table 2).

Lizards can be identified as re-captures because of the individual's number and pattern of clipped toes. The proportion of western fence lizards that were re-captured in 2009 was 29%. This very high proportion of re-captures may indicate that fence lizards are highly territorial, long lived, abundant, or are particularly detectable using pitfall traps. All of the other lizard species, with the exception of coastal whiptails (CNTI) and California horned lizard (PHCO), also had a high proportion of re-captures (range 12-16%).

The number of different species captured was lowest in the winter months (Table 4). These months in southern California are typically wet and cold (Figure 6). These conditions were generally favorable for capturing amphibians, particularly black-bellied slender salamanders, however most other species were caught less frequently during these periods (Table 4). Lizard species, such as western fence lizard (SCOC) and western skink (EUSK) were captured in higher numbers in the grass and woodland sites (Figure 9).

Species that were not captured at all or were rarely captured in the Malibu watershed pitfall arrays, are assumed to be rare in the sampling location's habitat, rare in the entire SMMNRA, or hard to detect with our capture methods. Some species like the California horned lizard prefer open sandy areas and are a species of special concern for the CADFG and USFWS, therefore they are probably rare within this sampling area. Some snake species, however, may be common in our area, but are not detectable with the current best trapping methods. For example, the southern pacific rattlesnake is often seen in the study area but was rarely captured.

Cabrillo National Monument

Lizard captures far outweighed snake or amphibian captures at CABR. The frequency with which we observe the five lizard species while working around the park is in line with the proportion of each species caught in the arrays; that is, fence lizards (SCOC) and side-blotched lizards (UTST) are the most commonly observed followed by orange-throated whiptails (CNHY) and alligator lizards (ELMU). Legless lizards (ANPU) are rarely observed. The recapture rate of approximately 25% for each of the four more common lizards at CABR suggests the arrays are catching lizards indiscriminately. These recapture rates are similar to the rate of fence lizard recaptures at SAMO, and the same conclusions may be applied at CABR.

Snakes are observed on a fairly regular basis at CABR. Only eight captures in the arrays suggests the arrays simply are not very good at catching snakes at CABR. However, they are useful in helping us at least document occurrence of the less common species, such as *Diadophus punctatus*.

Seasonal patterns in captures were evident at CABR. Fence lizards, whiptails, and alligator lizards were captured more frequently in the spring and early summer months. On Point Loma, these months are mild but much cooler than later in the summer. A strong marine layer tends to persist during the first half of the day during May, June, and even some of July. Hotter temperatures occur in August, September, and October.

Historically two lizard species and five snake species were known to occur on the Point Loma peninsula that were not captured or seen in 2009 (Table 8). In addition one snake species *Hypsiglena torquata* was detected (but not captured in an array) during the 1995-2001 surveys but not in 2009. This species is very rare and cryptic but could be present at CABR without having been caught in the arrays (Atkinson et al. 2003). Also, the introduced snake *Charina trivirgata* was not caught or seen in 2009 at CABR. Capture data from 2002 through 2008 for CABR exists but has not yet been analyzed. In addition, Atkinson et al. (2003) note that *Masticophis lateralis* appeared to be in decline on the Point Loma peninsula, and the decline may have been related to *El Nino* conditions. Future analyses should seek to answer whether *M. lateralis* has declined at CABR or fluctuated over time. However, it did at least occur within the CABR data in 2009.

Table 8. Herpetological species captured at CABR and known historically. See Atkinson et al. (2003) for records from 1995-2001 surveys and historical data.

Species	Common Name	2009 Survey	1995-2001 Surveys	Historical
Amphibians				
Batrachoseps pacificus	Pacific slender salamander	x	x	X
Lizards				
Anniella pulchra	Legless Lizard	x	x	X
Cnemidophorus hyperythrus	Orange-throated whiptail	x	x	X
Elgaria multicarinata	San Diego alligator lizard	x	x	X
Eumeces skiltonianus	Coronado skink			X
Phynosoma coronatum	Coast horned lizard			X
Sceloporus occidentalis	Great Basin fence lizard	x	x	X
Uta stansburiana	California side-blotched lizard	x	x	X
Snakes				
Arizona elegans	California glossy snake			X
Charina trivirgata	Coastal rosy boa		x (introduced)	
Coluber constrictor	Yellow-bellied racer			X
Crotalus exsul	Red diamond rattlesnake			X
Crotalus viridis	Southern Pacific rattlesnake	x	x	X
Diadophis punctatus	Western ringneck snake	x	x	x
Hypsiglena torquata	Night snake		x	x
Lampropeltis getula	California kingsnake	x	x	x
Masticophis flagellum	Coachwhip/red racer			x
Masticophis lateralis	California striped racer	x	x	x
Pituophis melanoleucas	Gopher snake	x	x	x
Rhinocheilus lecontei	Long-nose snake			x

Channel Island National Park

CHIS monitoring data provides indices of abundance (population indices) for one to a few transects per monitored island. Population indices can be compared between years to detect trends in abundance of island lizard and amphibian species. In addition, surveys on Santa Barbara Island provide interesting and valuable data on the island night lizard, a unique island endemic. In general, heavier night lizards had longer snout-vent lengths. This trend was similar for the other lizard species, and slender salamanders.

On San Miguel Island, all three species (slender salamanders, fence lizards, and alligator lizards) were caught at 2 of the 3 sites. However, at one site (Nidever Canyon), only the slender salamander was captured. In the future, it would be interesting to examine habitat differences between these sampling sites.

Summary and Future directions

This analysis was useful in identifying ways to improve the existing protocols and to strategically shift sampling to improve the power to detect trends in occupancy or abundance indices. For example, it may be advantageous to forego sampling in certain habitats during winter months and use those field hours during a different month or habitat. Furthermore, all three parks are currently using a sampling design that relies on judgement sampling, which means there is no statistical inference to the larger study area.

We are currently revising the sampling design for SAMO to incorporate a probabilistic sampling design as well as refining the data analysis methods for evaluating long-term trends in occupancy. The sampling design and analysis methods for CABR and CHIS should be revised in the near future as well. The CHIS herpetofauna monitoring program could be improved by increasing the number of samples (transect), or possibly using a different capture technique. Mark-recapture of the larger lizard species would help to estimate detection probabilities. The collection of covariate data such as precipitation and temperature should also be carefully considered. We suggest that future reports evaluate temperature, rainfall, habitat type, and month of data collection as covariates to examine trends in occupancy and abundance of herpetofauna at all three parks within the Mediterranean Coast Network. Demographic data (sex, size, etc.) along with recapture data should also be analyzed in future periodic trend reports.

Literature Cited

Atkinson, A. J., R. N. Fisher, C. J. Rochester, and C. W. Brown. 2003. Sampling design optimization and establishment of baselines for herpetofauna arrays at the Point Loma Ecological Reserve. U.S.Geological Survey, Western Ecological Research Center, San Diego, California.

Austin, G. 1996. Terrestrial vertebrate monitoring, Channel Islands National Park, 1995 annual report. Channel Islands National Park Technical Report CHIS-96-04. National Park Service, Ventura, California. 18 pp.

Austin, G. 1998. Terrestrial vertebrate monitoring, Channel Islands National Park, 1996 annual report. Channel Islands National Park Technical Report 98-02. National Park Service, Ventura, California. 22 pp.

Blaustein, A. R., and D. B. Wake. 1990. Declining amphibian populations: a global phenomenon? *Trends in Ecology and Evolution* 5:203-204.

Brown, C. W., and R. N. Fisher. 2002. Inventory and management needs study of Point Loma herpetofauna (reptiles and amphibians) with comments on mammals and invertebrates, 2001. Technical Report, U.S.Geological Survey.

Busteed, G., J. L. Cameron, M. Robertson, S. P. D. Riley, L. Lee, A. Compton, E. Berbeo, and T. Duffield. 2006. Monitoring of Terrestrial Reptiles & Amphibians in the Mediterranean Coast Network: Santa Monica Mountains & Cabrillo National Monument, Version 1.0. Natural Resources Technical Report NPS/MEDN/NRTR—2006/005. National Park Service, Thousand Oaks, California.

Campbell, H. W., and S. P. Christman. 1982. Field techniques for herpetofaunal community analysis. Pages 193-200 *in* N. J. Scott, editor. Herpetofaunal communities. Wildlife Research Report 13. U. S. D. I. Fish and Wildlife Service, Washington D.C.

Case, T. J., and R. N. Fisher. 2001. Measuring and predicting species presence: coastal sage scrub case study. Pages 47-71 *in* M. Hunsaker, M. Goodchild, M. Friedl, and T. J. Case, editors. Uncertainty in spatial data for ecology. Springer-Verlag Press, Berlin.

Corn, P. S. 1994. Straight-line drift fences and pitfall traps. Pages 109-117 *in* W. B. Heyer, M. A. Donnelly, R. W. McDiarmid, L. C. Hayek, and M. S. Foster, editors. Measuring and monitoring biological diversity: standard methods for amphibians. Smithsonian Institution Press, Washington, D. C.

De Lisle, H. G., G. Gilbert, J. Feldner, P. O'Connor, M. Peterson, and P. Brown 1986. The distribution and present status of the Herpetofauna of the Santa Monica Mountains of Los Angeles and Ventura Counties, California. Southwest Herpetologist Society, Los Angeles, California.

Enge, K. M. 2001. The pitfalls of pitfall traps. *Journal of Herpetology* 35:467-478.

Fellers, G. M., C.A. Drost, and B.W. Arnold. 1988. Terrestrial Vertebrate Monitoring Handbook. Channel Islands National Park, Ventura, California. 60 pp.

Fisher, R. N., and T. J. Case. 2000a. Distribution of the herpetofauna of coastal southern California with reference to elevation effects. . Pages 137-144 *in* J. E. Keeley, M. Baer-Keeley, and C. J. Fotheringham, editors. 2nd Interface between Ecology and Land Development in California. U.S. Geological Survey, Sacramento, CA.

Fisher, R. N., and T. J. Case. 2000b. Southern California herpetofauna research and monitoring: 1995-1999 data summation report. Southern California Fish & Game, Carlsbad, California and California U.S. Fish & Wildlife Service, Sacramento, California.

Fisher, R. N., A. V. Suarez, and T. J. Case. 2002. Spatial patterns in the abundance of the coastal horned lizard. *Conservation Biology* 16:205-215.

Fitch, H. S. 1992. Methods of sampling snake populations and their relative success. *Herpetological Review* 23:17-19.

Gamradt, S. C., and L. B. Kats. 1996. Effect of introduced crayfish and mosquito fish on California newts. *Conservation Biology* 10:1155-1162.

Gamradt, S. C., and L. B. Kats. 1997. Impact of chaparral fire-induced sedimentation on ovoposition of stream-breeding California newts (*Taricha torosa*). *Oecologia* 110:546-549.

Greenberg, C. H., D. G. Neary, and L. D. Harris. 1994. A comparison of herpetofaunal sampling effectiveness of pitfall, single-ended, and double-ended funnel traps used with drift fences. *Journal of Herpetology* 28:319-324.

Schwemm, C.A. 1995. Terrestrial vertebrate monitoring, Channel Islands National Park, 1993 annual report. Channel Islands National Park Technical Report CHIS-94-02. National Park Service, Ventura, California. 44 pp.

Schwemm, C.A. 1996. Terrestrial vertebrate monitoring, Channel Islands National Park, 1994 annual report. Channel Islands National Park Technical Report CHIS-96-03. National Park Service, Ventura, California. 30 pp.

Sinervo, B., F. Méndez-de-la-Cruz, D. B. Miles, B. Heulin, E. Bastiaans, M. V.-S. Cruz, R. Lara-Resendiz, N. Martínez-Méndez, M. L. Calderón-Espinosa, R. N. Meza-Lázaro, H. Gadsden, L. J. Avila, M. Morando, I. J. D. l. Riva, P. V. Sepulveda, C. F. D. Rocha, N. Ibargüengoytía, C. A. Puntriano, M. Massot, V. Lepetz, T. A. Oksanen, D. G. Chapple, A. M. Bauer, W. R. Branch, J. Clobert, and J. Jack W. Sites. 2010. Erosion of lizard diversity by climate change and altered thermal niches. *Science* 328:894-899.

Stokes, D. C., C. J. Rochester, R. N. Fisher, and T. J. Case. 2001. DRAFT Herpetological monitoring using pitfall trapping design in southern California. Open File Report, U.S. Geological Survey.